Understanding Adolescence for Girls:
A Body-Positive Guide to Puberty

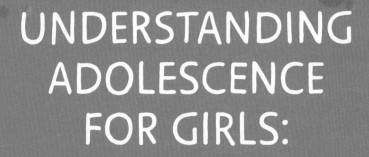

UNDERSTANDING ADOLESCENCE FOR GIRLS:

A Body-Positive Guide to Puberty

By Barbara Pietruszczak
Illustrated by Anna Rudak

Translated from the Polish by
Agnes Monod-Gayraud

Arctis

W1-Media, Inc.
Arctis Books USA
Stamford, CT, USA

Original title: Twoje ciałopozytywne dojrzewanie.
Przewodnik po zmianach w ciele, pierwszej miesiączce i ciałopozytywności.
Text: Barbara Pietruszczak
Illustrations and cover design: Anna Rudak
Text © copyright by moonka 2021
Illustrations © copyright by moonka 2021

First hardcover English edition published by
W1-Media Inc. / Arctis Books USA 2024

Visit our website at www.arctis-books.com

1 3 5 7 9 8 6 4 2

The Library of Congress Control Number: 2024930611
ISBN 978-1-64690-041-1
English translation copyright © Agnes Monod-Gayraud, 2024

Printed in China

MIX
Paper | Supporting
responsible forestry
FSC® C020056

Dedicated to all girls
around the world

Table of Contents:

Introduction

Hi! My name is Barbara. As a journalist, my job is all about writing, reading, and talking to people about the most interesting things in the world. When I'm drawn in by a certain topic, I get really invested. And it turns out that the human body is the subject that has fascinated me the most.

I'm completely in awe of what our bodies allow us to do and all the ways bodily functions connect to our thoughts and feelings. I've found that the knowledge of our own bodies is a superpower because it helps us understand what's going on inside of us. This is especially true during adolescence—a time of big changes.

Sometimes these changes happen so fast that we feel like we can hardly keep up. It can also feel like we have to figure out our bodies and how they work from scratch. This is exactly why I wrote this book—to help you understand what puberty and adolescence are about. To help you get to know your body ... and yourself! And to accompany you on the path to feeling good in your own skin.

I hope that this book will be a useful and joyful guide to this remarkable period in your life.

Barbara

How to Use This Book

It's all up to you, really. You might want to read it on your own, or maybe you'd like to go through it with someone by your side. It's your call.

You might find that there might be some things you don't understand right away—be sure to ask a parent, guardian, or someone else you trust for more info.

If there are any words related to the body that you don't understand—feel free to take a look at the anatomical diagrams and captions in Chapter 6.

This book is focused on the way a girl goes through puberty. But it's obvious that some people reading this book might not be girls. Some readers, as a matter of fact, might not identify as girls, but they might still be going through many of the changes described in this book. Feel free to take only what you find useful from this book.

Try not to rush through it. There's a whole lot of information in these pages. You might want to read it in small bursts and concentrate on the parts that interest you the most. Unless, of course, you prefer reading a book all the way from cover to cover. It's up to you how you want to engage with it.

One last thing—if you want to make notes and doodle all over this book, go right ahead. Underline and highlight whatever you find you'd like to pay special attention to. I really enjoy marking up my books with the things that are especially interesting or important to me ... In fact, I tend to scribble quite a bit in the margins of my books. But all of that is up to you!

CHAPTER 1

Welcome Home!

Your body is your shelter. You inhabit every bit of it. From your pinkie toe to your belly button. From the top of your head to your toes and your gut, lungs, and throat. Every beauty mark and freckle, every scar—it's all you! Entirely perfect, inimitable, and unique in every way.

You are your body. It's the machine that lets you jump, run, write, and sing. It lets you taste the flavor of a yummy piece of cake, smell the flowers, and feel the warmth of a hug. It lets you read, feel the rays of the sun on your skin, and swim.

This affirmational approach to the body is what we call body positivity. In other words, it's a respectful and appreciative understanding of the skin we're in.

This book will show you different ways you can find and develop your own understanding of body positivity.

Let's start with a simple exercise.
Can you list some things your body gives you the ability to do? You can think about these things and list them on the opposite page. Try to include not only the things you enjoy doing most but also some of the very basic things you do every day. This list will be useful to come back to when you find yourself forgetting (and we all do sometimes) the reasons why your body is so wonderful.

Things I'm able to do thanks to my body:

. . . .

. . . .

. . . .

. . . .

. . . .

. . . .

. . . .

. . . .

. . . .

. . . .

Our bodies are made up of tiny building blocks we call cells. These cells come together to create our bones, brains, blood, skin, hair, and everything else—even our immune systems!

Cells come in a variety of shapes and sizes, depending on their purpose. Some look like tiny doughnuts (such as red blood cells) and others like kites (such as the cells of the nervous system).

All of these cells are so small that you can only see them under a microscope. The largest of all is the egg released by the ovaries—and we'll definitely come back to that one a bit later on.

Did you know . . .

There are bits of this world even smaller than a cell! The entire universe—including the planets, comets, the moon, and the Earth—are made up of the same little pieces, which we call atoms. Your body is entirely made up of atoms, so we can even say that you are made of stardust!

Inside our bodies, everything is interconnected: Feelings and emotions have an effect on how you feel both physically and mentally—even impacting your energy levels. Aches, pains, and illnesses, especially in the long term, have an effect on how you feel. Feelings of sadness or anxiety might make your stomach hurt. Anger might end up feeling like a headache, while joy can make you feel like you're lighter than air. Take a moment to listen to yourself—and your body—whenever you need to.

CHAPTER 2

What Is Puberty?

Puberty is a time when your body goes through a major renovation and a lot of things get switched around. In other words, it's a real revolution, led by Mother Nature herself! And the whole purpose of these physical and psychological changes is to take a human being from childhood into adulthood.

We refer to this process as puberty—or adolescence. It's something both girls and boys go through, but it happens in entirely different ways for either gender.

In girls, puberty typically occurs between 8 and 13 years old and lasts from about 3 to 6 years.

This is a time when your body will begin to go through quite substantial changes that can also be quite intense. At the same time, you will feel like all of you is changing, meaning your thoughts and emotions, too ... such as how you see yourself and others or the way you think about the world.

Did you know . . .

In many cultures throughout the world, puberty is a partic-
ularly important time, and that's why it's often celebrated
through a plethora of different ceremonies. These rituals
are meant to separate the experience of childhood from
adulthood. Typically, the child leaves their immediate family

and community for a few weeks or months, and in this time, the elders teach them important lessons and set them up for various trials to test their maturity and resilience. When that person goes through all the trials successfully, they are considered an adult at last. When they return home, they are welcomed with enormous fanfare and a party that has everyone dancing all night long.

Among the Venda tribe of South Africa, girls who have already had their first period spend three months learning about marriage, sexuality, pregnancy, and childbirth. In this culture, the python is a symbol of fertility, which is why the final event of this "rite of passage" is the "dance of the python" that goes on for hours. This is how the tribe celebrates their coming of age and the changes that are part of the package.

This is definitely an important moment in your life. In fact, it's a lot like the first part of a great expedition. And so, it does help (as for any of life's expeditions) to be prepared. Now, let's have a look at the map of where we're heading, shall we?

Step-by-step map
What's actually going on here . . .

Ages 7–11

Hello, it's the time for hormones to shine! The pituitary gland releases hormones that manage the body's development, sending the message to the ovaries to start growing and produce their own helping of hormones.

Puberty: Ready, set, go!

Ages 9–14

Growth spurt time! Your body begins to develop even more intensively than before—and you'll find yourself growing faster than ever, especially in the year just before your first period. A girl can grow up to three inches in just over 12 months!

This is also when the breasts start to develop in a process called "budding."

GROWTH SPURT

AGES 9 – 14

BREASTS BEGINNING TO BUD

Ages 9 – 14

Ages 10–16

It starts to get a bit hairy at this point, with leg hair getting a bit darker and sometimes thicker. Hair also starts appearing in other places, such as under the arms and around the vulva, which is between the legs. This usually starts happening a year or two after the breasts have begun to bud.

Ages 9–16

This is when a girl can expect to get her first period! It usually comes about two years after the breasts have started to develop.

The growth spurt spurred on by adolescence begins to slow down. After getting their first period, girls tend to grow an average of about four inches taller.

Ages 13–18

Let's take it from the top! As the brain grows and develops, you'll also find you're starting to think about your emotions and relationships in a different way. Your thought processes are getting more complex, and you find yourself making more intricate observations and considering more complex ideas. Of your whole body, the brain is the organ that takes the longest to develop—it doesn't reach full maturity until you're 25 years old!

Now we'll go through each stage step by step to make it all clearer and more comprehensive.

Ready? Let's go!

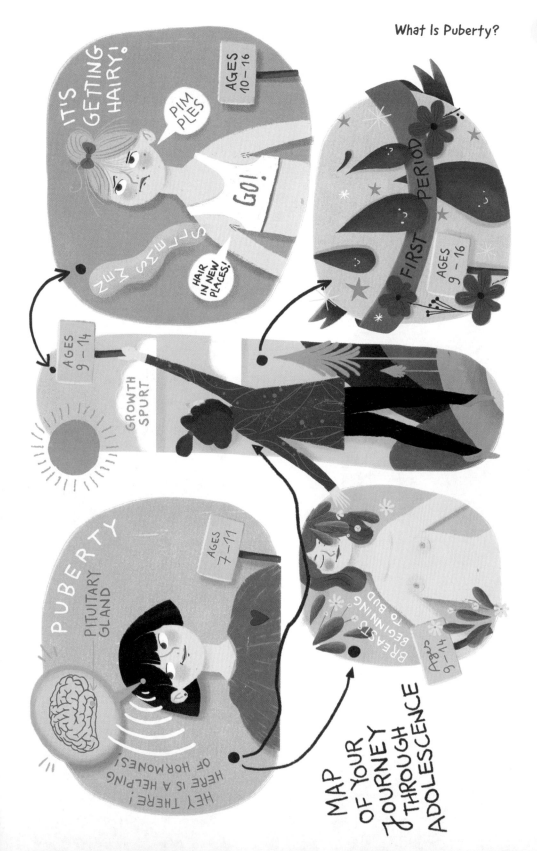

CHAPTER 3

The Changes I'm Going Through

Puberty begins with an event that is entirely invisible to the naked eye: The pituitary gland deep in the brain is activated and begins to produce hormones that launch the process of puberty. These remarkable chemicals act like couriers, traveling via the bloodstream to deliver important messages to the body's many cells and organs that tell them exactly what (or what not) to do.

These hormones travel all the way from the brain to the lower abdomen, alerting the ovaries (tiny organs we will talk more about in the next few pages) that it's time to wake up and start growing . . . and producing other types of hormones! The specific chemicals produced by the ovaries are referred to as sex hormones.

These hormones surge through the whole body with a very important goal—to deliver important instructions for the next steps necessary for setting puberty into motion. And these hormones are the key to initiating these big changes!

Everything's growing

To say that you're shooting up like a weed is an understatement. The onset of puberty begins with a sudden growth spurt. Throughout your whole life, you've experienced such an intense period of growth only once before—when you were two! Now, you might grow as many as four inches taller in a single year!

> **Let's remember that each person develops at their own pace.**

Not everybody goes through a sudden and extreme growth spurt. Some people grow more slowly and over a longer period of time. And some people start growing earlier than others—in fact, girls tend to experience the first hints of puberty faster than boys.

Facial features

It's not just the body that's going through puberty—the face is also going through its own set of changes. Noses get bigger, the forehead gets wider, and the chin becomes more pronounced. The entire face begins to transform into a more adult version of you.

But not all at once!

Certain body parts may develop at a different pace than the rest. It usually starts with the hands and feet getting bigger. Your parents might even wonder how you've already grown out of a pair of shoes they bought you a few months ago. The arms and legs can grow faster than the rest of the body, which might make you feel like a daddy longlegs spider for a little while.

Incredible changes

Puberty is a time when most people start to feel a little different. This is a time of exciting changes, but it can also feel unsettling, confusing, uncomfortable, or even downright weird. The good news is that these changes happen gradually, so you have plenty of time to get used to the changes and begin to get to know this new adolescent version of yourself.

Yes, your body is perfectly equipped to carry out the changes that are a natural part of puberty. Trust your body and let it lead the way.

Body shapes

Apart from getting taller and bigger overall, you might notice your hips also getting wider. The bones of the pelvis expand until they achieve the adequate width for an adult woman. A woman's pelvis is wider than that of a man so that—if one day she decides she wants to become a mother—her body is better prepared to carry a child and give birth.

Other parts of your body might start to change as well—the belly, buttocks, and legs getting curvier thanks to an extra layer of fat tissue that allows women to store more energy overall than men do. This stored energy proves useful if a woman decides to become pregnant—or finds herself facing a Hunger Games–style challenge. The body's fat stores are also essential in the royal realm of hormonal regulation, which controls many bodily processes.

In spite of the fact that every girl goes through a similar process on the way to becoming a woman, the process doesn't always look the same for everybody. After all, we're all unique, and even as adults, there are so many differences that make each woman experience a different embodiment of womanhood, no matter their age. Some women are statuesque and curvy, some are short and slender, others are tall and slim as a reed, and others are short with wide hips and have either small or full breasts. We all have our individual shapes, and that's exactly how it's supposed to be.

There's not one single body type to fit all the different women and girls of the world.

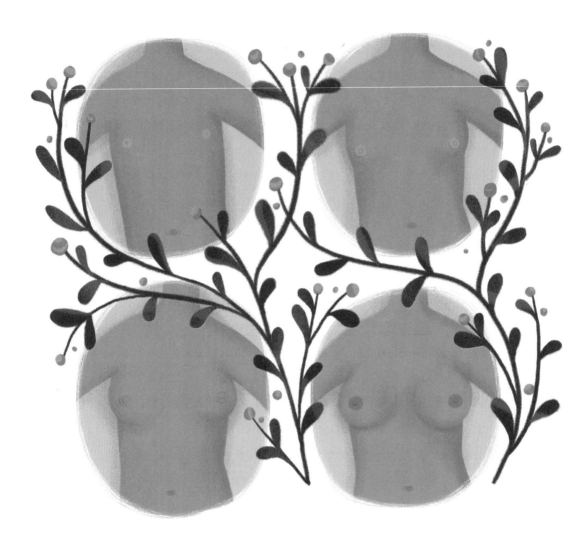

Breasts

The first sign of puberty is when breasts start to develop. It's sort of like the first inkling of spring—a subtle hint of the vibrant changes that are about to bloom.

In other words, you are truly the first one who's going to notice when things start to happen. Around the nipples, you'll start to feel some bumps, and they could even feel a bit tender or painful. This usually happens between the ages of 9 and 14. Every girl experiences this at a different time, and when their breasts begin to grow, they will eventually end up being all different sizes. **Even adult women often have one breast bigger than the other.** Overall, it can take three or more years for breasts to fully develop. It's very much an individual thing.

Let's keep in mind that every individual develops at their own pace. Your body is smart, and it knows exactly what it's doing.

Why are some breasts small and some quite big?

The size and shape of someone's breasts usually depend on genetics. This means you are likely to have the same size and shape of breasts as other women in your family: for instance, your mother, grandmother, sister, or aunt.

When a woman decides she wants to have a baby, it doesn't matter how big or little her breasts are. All sorts are suitable for breastfeeding—every kind of breast has the potential to produce milk.

The shape of the breast can change throughout a woman's life, depending on a large number of factors, which may include fluctuations in weight, pregnancy and breastfeeding, the effects of time and gravity, and hormonal changes.

What's the point of having breasts?

Women develop breasts mainly for the purpose of producing milk and feeding their offspring. This is a natural process for all mammals, in other words, animals that are born from their mother and drink milk for the first few months of life. We're basically like cats and dogs in that respect!

Breastmilk is considered to be an optimal food for a newborn human. When a woman is pregnant, the breast tissue is already becoming prepared for producing milk so that as soon as a child is born, they can start breastfeeding and receive the nutrition required to continue growing and developing. Of course, some women either find it difficult or even impossible to breastfeed. Fortunately, there are alternative milk products on the market to sustain their babies.

Have you ever heard of nursemaids?

In the past, people would sometimes hire a woman to breastfeed another family's child (typically, such families were quite rich) because the mother was not willing or able to feed the baby herself. It could also be the case that the mother wanted to have another baby soon after—and breastfeeding generally makes it less likely for a woman to become pregnant.

Getting back to the topic of nipples

As soon as the breasts begin to grow, you might notice that the nipples also start changing (including the areola, which is the skin around the nipple). They might become more prominent, stick out more, or change color. It's also possible for little hairs to grow around the nipple. **This is all completely normal.**

There are so many kinds of nipples in the world, but even many adults don't realize how different nipples can be. This is probably because a lot of magazines and movies only show a few kinds of nipples—which are usually stiff and perky. This is only one of the many ways nipples can appear since they are typically soft and relaxed—unless responding to a stimulus like cold or touch.

My first bra

A lot of girls and women choose to wear a bra because they find it comfortable as they begin to develop breasts. It can provide support for the breasts, especially when they feel a bit heavy—or if they feel that they get in the way when playing sports. **Choosing a well-fitting bra can also help take some pressure off of your back.**

What are the other benefits of wearing a bra? In the winter, a bra can definitely add a layer of warmth—especially since the breasts stick out (like the nose and ears), which makes them more susceptible to colder temperatures.

When you start feeling your breasts getting bigger, you might feel like it's time to go out and get your first bra. It's natural to be curious about what it feels like to wear one. If you feel like it's the right time, reach out to someone you trust—your mom, dad, or another person you trust. You can go shopping together, either ordering a few bras online or shopping at a physical store.

It's up to the individual to decide whether they want to wear a bra or not. Some women find it entirely useless to wear a bra, while other women find it essential. Many women take pleasure in wearing lacy bras and lingerie. **We're all different, and that's what makes life interesting!**

How do I figure out my bra size?

40D or 32A? It's not quite a game of Battleship, but a game of bra sizes instead. The letter is meant to indicate the cup size. In other words, the bigger the breasts, the larger the cup size. And the number refers to the circumference around the rib cage just below the breasts—in inches.

Some girls find it useful to wear a bra on a daily basis. When you run or jump, you'll notice your breasts moving around, too—not everybody finds this feeling comfortable, so wearing a sports bra can help keep things in place. Most shops stock bras in standard sizes from extra-small sizes to extra-large ones. The most important thing is for the bra to feel comfortable. If it feels too tight, it's best to size up. There are also special shops where they do "bra fittings," which means that the salesperson is trained to find you the right size and style based on some measurements.

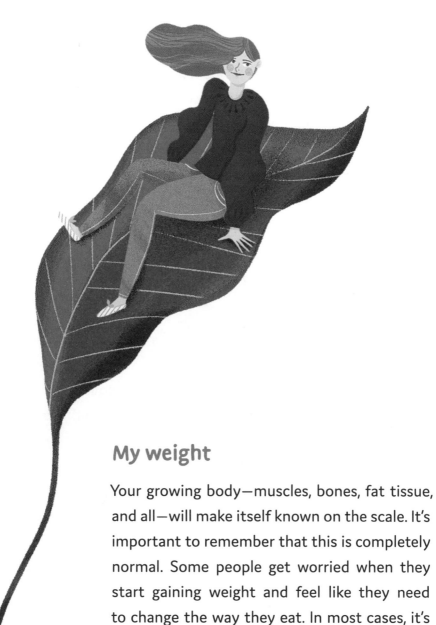

My weight

Your growing body—muscles, bones, fat tissue, and all—will make itself known on the scale. It's important to remember that this is completely normal. Some people get worried when they start gaining weight and feel like they need to change the way they eat. In most cases, it's completely unnecessary to adjust your food intake. Your growing body needs nutritious food!

Another important point is that weight gain isn't always tied to food intake—it can also be related to a hormonal imbalance or limited physical activity. If you do feel concerned about your weight (because either you feel like maybe you would like to weigh a bit more or a bit less), talk to your parents about it. You can meet with your doctor together to make sure everything is in order.

Stretch marks

When people go through growth spurts, sometimes their skin has a hard time keeping up. After all, the skin has to stretch pretty quickly to do its job and cover a whole growing body. This is why stretch marks sometimes appear on the hips, buttocks, thighs, back, or other places on the body. These stretch marks look like tiny pink or white stripes on the skin, forming in areas where the skin has "stretched" to accommodate a growth spurt. These stripes can also appear on the breasts and belly—and not just during puberty. Sudden weight loss or gain, pregnancy, or intensive workouts can make stretch marks appear—on both male and female bodies. And a lot of people celebrate the "tiger stripes" that make them unique.

Cellulite

This is a layer of body fat that naturally takes on a wavy texture and can appear on the thighs, buttocks, belly, or upper arms—or all of the above.

Cellulite is completely normal, and most women and men have some cellulite somewhere on their bodies.

Magazines and television shows have managed to convince a lot of people that cellulite is a flaw. Companies make money off of this insecurity by promoting products that are meant to "fight" or get rid of it. When we hear stuff like this, we should remember that our bodies are never our enemies and there is never any need to "fight" it.

Sebum, zits, and all that good stuff

Our skin contains an assortment of glands, which are tiny organs that produce a range of substances our bodies need, such as tears, sweat, and sebum. Some of these glands aren't activated until puberty begins, including the sebum glands.

Sebum is an oily substance meant to protect and condition the skin so that it can be well moisturized and supple. As you grow up, your body gradually learns to adjust the amount of sebum it produces, so it can often be the case that sometimes it produces way more than necessary. As a result, your skin and hair can feel quite oily. Sebum may also plug the skin's pores (tiny openings in the skin that allow sebum and other substances to rise to the surface) and cause pimples to form. As gross as it may feel, this is a normal part of puberty. Zits tend to break out on the face, but they may also appear on the chest or back. It's usually best not to pick them but instead simply wash them with a gentle cleanser. It can be quite frustrating, but the best treatment for pimples is patience because picking at them could cause scars.

However, if you have a whole lot of pimples and they are causing significant discomfort or pain, it's a good idea to check in with a dermatologist—a doctor specializing in skin conditions.

Let's not forget that pimples and redness are normal. Sometimes, when the skin feels itchy and irritated, it's hard to think about anything else. But other people still see *you*—the same lovely person you are and who they enjoy being around—and the pimples are never as awful as they seem.

Pimples do tend to come and go—even adults get them sometimes! Pimples are just a part of life, and most of us have to deal with them at one time or another.

It's the pits!

Sweat glands are like tiny tunnels that transport sweat to the surface of the skin. We have sweat glands all over our bodies, but they're concentrated in certain places like the feet, hands, and head.

Getting sweaty often is a natural part of puberty.

You'll start to notice yourself getting a bit sweatier when it's hot or when you're active, but also when you're feeling more emotional—nervous, afraid, excited, or even angry. You might feel sweatier in your armpits and around the pubic area. It's all completely normal and not something to worry about.

Adolescent sweat also has a different smell—you might find it a bit more pungent, perhaps, than when you were a child. When people get hot and sweaty, sometimes that sweat has a certain smell that comes about when the bacteria living on your skin start to multiply in that warm and damp environment. The more they multiply, the more a person might start to smell different. Once again, all this is normal and part of growing up. There are different ways people can avoid getting too smelly, starting with a daily shower and soap. There are also various deodorants (that cover up the smell of your sweat with a more pleasant scent or contain ingredients that reduce the amount of bacteria on the skin) and antiperspirants (that limit the production or release of sweat). Ask an adult for advice on which type works for them and see if any of them suit you.

The best solution for extra-sweaty armpits is a shower and fresh underwear every day.

It's getting hairy

As we grow up, we start to notice a lot more hair growing in unexpected places. Sometimes it's a little bunch of hair, or other times it's a lone "pioneer" surveying the terrain before other little hairs join in.

During puberty, you'll notice new bunches of hair growing under the arms and around the pubic area (called "pubic hairs"). These hairs start growing on the front of the pubis, between the legs, and all the way to the rear end. Sometimes there's even a trail leading up to the belly button! The main job of these patches of hair is to protect these sensitive areas from rubbing and irritation.

You might also see hair getting a bit thicker in other places, such as the eyebrows or above the upper lip, as well as the arms, legs, and feet. Puberty, along with all the hormones that direct its progression, can also make hairs grow out of beauty spots and moles. Little hairs can also start growing around the nipples.

These new hairs might be the same color as the hair on your head, but they can also be lighter or darker. Every person is different, and no two bodies will ever look the same.

Did you know . . .

It's only recently that people started getting rid of some of their body hair. Even 40 years ago, a lot of people living in Europe and America didn't tend to shave their armpits, legs, or pubic areas. It wasn't until fashion and lifestyle magazines started publishing images of hairless bodies that people decided they wanted to get rid of their body hair, and corporations leaped at the chance to sell people more razors and other hair-removal products. A lot of the female bodies shown in movies, television, advertisements, and even Instagram and TikTok appear hairless.

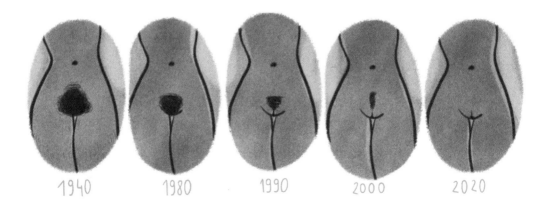

1940   1980   1990   2000   2020

So, it can start to feel like all women and girls have to be hairless too! But that's complete nonsense! Women have a right to decide what they want to do with their bodies, and that includes choosing whether or not to remove their body hair. The most important thing is to be aware that you're doing it for yourself—if a girl decides to wax or shave her legs, it should be because she wants to, not because she feels pressured by other people. And it's not always easy to make that distinction.

For a lot of women I know, it took some time for them to figure out what they wanted to do. Some people don't remove any of their body hair at all, while some of them only do it in the summer. Some only shave the hair on their calves, and some get laser hair removal on their entire legs. And some of them never shave their armpits. What you decide to do with your body hair is entirely your business!

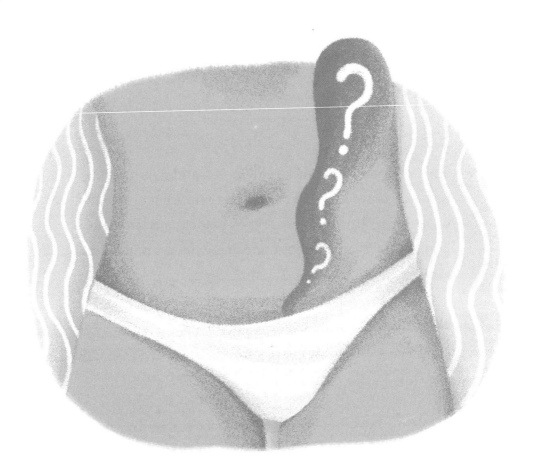

What's going on down there?

There are plenty of words to describe the parts that make up the pubic area, including vagina or vulva, but you may have your own words to describe them. The vagina is a canal that stretches from the vulva, located right behind the urethra (the hole we use to pee). You'll find out more about the vagina later in this book.

Vulva, labia, genitalia, or privates. Whatever you choose to call them, these are the external sex organs. In other words, these are the parts you see and feel on the outside of your body. The most important thing is for you to use the word that makes you feel the most comfortable.

Sometimes, you might notice some light discharge in your underwear. It's absolutely nothing to be worried about—it's simply an indication that your body is going through a series of changes to prepare for your first menstrual period.

When you do start menstruating, your vagina will start producing different types of discharge—sometimes it will be runny like egg whites, and other days it might appear thicker and more creamy. It's all normal!

When you get accustomed to your monthly cycle, you might notice correlations between each particular phase and the type of discharge you see.

You will also notice that your vagina will have a different smell on certain days. This is also completely normal, and it's good to take note of your personal scent so that you can be aware if it changes drastically in any way, which can be an indication that something is off.

It's important to remember that a vagina is supposed to smell like a vagina—it's not supposed to smell like a bouquet of flowers. You don't need any special products to clean your pubic area—soap and water are enough to keep the area fresh and clean. It's also good to remember that only the external genital area needs washing. The vagina (which is the internal part of the genitals) doesn't require any kind of bathing because it is designed to clean itself!

Are you ready to continue to the next destination on our journey? It's time to find out how to get yourself prepared for puberty in a way that makes you feel comfortable and positive about your changing body.

CHAPTER 4

Let's Power Up!

As you go through puberty, people might start looking at you differently, and they might make comments about the changes you're going through.

Just a while ago you were a child, and now you're becoming a woman.

These comments can come from other kids or adults. Sometimes these comments might be polite and kind, making you feel quite good about yourself. Other times, they can make you feel uncomfortable or even hurt. It's important to remember that inappropriate comments have nothing to do with you and everything to do with the person making them. It is up to the people around you to be responsible with their words—especially when talking to a child or an adolescent.

You have the right to refuse to let someone treat you in a way that makes you feel uncomfortable. And you have a right to be as vocal as you need to be to express this right. With practice, speaking up for yourself becomes easier and more natural. It's an important way of taking care of yourself and showing others that you have boundaries that shouldn't be crossed.

Let's take a look at
a couple of examples below . . .

1. At a birthday party, an aunt comes over
and says, right in front of everybody:
"Agnes, look how your boobies have grown!
You're becoming a little woman now!"

Agnes doesn't want to hear comments like that from
family members. She feels angry about her privacy being invaded. She can reply: "Auntie, this is my personal
business. I really don't appreciate you talking about me
like that."

🖋 **2. A friend tells Agnes:**

"You look ugly in that dress. I'd never go out in something like that."

She could say:

"Okay, well, it might not be your style, but I like the way I look in it."

🖋 **3. A guy on the street calls out:**

"Nice legs!"

Agnes ignores him but she still feels uncomfortable, and she tells her family about it when she gets home.

If someone you don't know tries to get your attention, it might not be the right time to speak out and set boundaries verbally. The most important thing is to make sure you are safe and comfortable, so often the best response *is* just to get away from that person quickly.

Every situation is different.
See how you feel at various moments
and allow yourself to trust these
feelings—they can help you figure out
what's good for you and what isn't.

Here is a space where you can practice various responses to certain types of uncomfortable situations:

. . . .

. . . .

. . . .

. . . .

. . . .

. . . .

. . . .

. . . .

. . . .

Let's talk a bit more about saying "no."

Girls can often have a harder time saying "no" and re-
fusing things than boys do. Sometimes adults end up
telling girls that they should be nice, polite, helpful, and
friendly, but this is a very old-fashioned view of the way
girls "should" be. Girls don't "need" to be a certain way in
order for people to like them. Girls should feel confident
to speak their minds and do what they feel they should
do. It's also important to know how to express your opin-
ion and protect your own interests. And sometimes that
means having to say "no" to someone.

So, make sure you get used to listening to yourself.

Too many women and girls don't have a knack of trusting
their gut instinct when it comes to troubling situations.
They might let themselves believe that it was only something trivial. But it's so important to know how to stop
for a moment and check your feelings. You can even tell
yourself, "What just happened wasn't okay. And I didn't
imagine it. I have the right to feel sad/angry/manipu-
lated."

This is true both for random comments and actions from strangers as well as from friends and relatives. Trust yourself and what you're feeling in the moment.

IMPORTANT:
Don't hold harsh feelings or experiences inside. Make sure you share things that are troubling you with someone close—optimally, an adult you can trust.

Your body is wonderful. And it only belongs to you.

Remember: No one has a right to touch your body without your permission! Not your private parts (vulva, buttocks, vagina, breasts) or any body part—even a single toe—if you don't want them to!

CHAPTER 5

How We See Ourselves

Have you ever thought about what an
incredible ability it is to see the world around us?
Have you thought about the biology that
makes it possible? Of course, you need eyes
to see . . . but they're only the first stop on the
way to perceiving what's in front of you.

The image of what you see in front of you is actually created in your mind. The eyes simply deliver vital information to the brain that allows it to recreate what you are seeing. Let's test out how this works: Stretch out the pointer finger of your right hand straight in front of you. Keep looking at it while you close one eye and then the other. Depending on which eye is open, you will see your finger from a slightly different angle. It isn't until you have both eyes open that the brain can combine that information to create a full picture of what you are seeing. But that's not all! Other factors can affect how we see things, including our thoughts and feelings. Imagine you have a friend who adores rats (and you happen to detest them) and the both of you are looking at a little picture of some baby rats. What looks like the most adorable thing in the world to her might look absolutely awful to you. And while you may appreciate how well the photographer captured the image, you don't want to look at it for too long. You're just not a big fan of rats, that's all.

So, even though you and your friend happen to be looking at the exact same thing, you both see and experience it a bit differently.

This is why we often say that people have a pair of **"invisible glasses"** perched on their noses (or, rather, their brains) through which we see the world. For instance, have you ever heard of the expression "rose-tinted glasses" to describe someone with a pretty optimistic approach to life? These glasses are made up of our thoughts, feelings, sensibilities, knowledge, experiences, and observations. And the combination of all these things can be drastically different from person to person.

Just think—perhaps one day you just might start thinking rats aren't so bad after all . . . and you might start to see that picture of baby rats in a whole new way!

What is body image?

Each person's body image is the picture we have in our minds of our bodies that is shaped by our thoughts and feelings. When someone feels good in their own skin and is happy with themselves, they typically have a positive body image. But when someone's mind is full of unpleasant thoughts about themselves and what they look like, this can lead to a negative body image.

A person's body image can fluctuate throughout their life. The good news is that you can actively shape your own body image by focusing on the positive.

Seeing through the eyes of other people

Do you ever think about how other people might see the world differently? There are lots of ways to try looking at things through other perspectives. Various types of media—books, movies, TV shows, magazines, and apps like Snapchat, Instagram, and TikTok—can reveal all the different ways that other people see the world.

One person's view might be fascinating and inspiring, but others can be misleading—or even damaging. The Internet is full of all different kinds of messages and posts. Some users insist on convincing their followers that certain people are better than others (when clearly that isn't true) or that the most important thing in the world is to try and look as beautiful as possible (when clearly each person has the right to decide what is most important to them).

Picture-perfect

What you see and hear around you can affect how you end up shaping your own body image—in other words, the way you see yourself. When you start to look at how other women talk about themselves, how they look, and how they behave, that might influence how you see yourself. This is perfectly normal. Even wolf cubs observe their mother to take cues on how to grow up into big wolves one day, too.

However, unlike wolf cubs, modern humans are sur-rounded by millions of different kinds of women and images of women: in the movies and on TV, ads, social media, and so on. It's enough to make your head spin! The trouble is that a lot of these images have little to do with reality. Most media outlets show a narrow segment of the female population—a woman who is typically slender, light-skinned, wearing makeup, and immaculately dressed in a seemingly never-ending col-lection of new designer clothing.

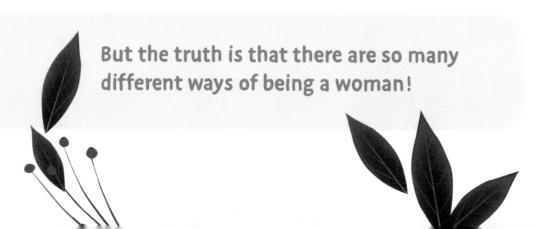

But the truth is that there are so many different ways of being a woman!

Not to mention the fact that so many of the images of girls and women in the media are edited or otherwise altered in some way. In other words, people use programs and apps to change their facial features or body shape in a photograph. It's as easy as adding a filter or pressing a button! So, a lot of the women we see in the media end up looking completely different in pictures than in real life. They often end up not looking like themselves at all!

When we spend a lot of time looking at these "idealized" images of women, it can start to put a strain on the way we see the world and ourselves. We might start to feel dissatisfied with our own appearance. This is why it's important to take care of ourselves and put more of an emphasis on building a positive and realistic body image.

So, how do you build a positive body image?

♥ Body positivity in practice

Focus on what your body can do and how much joy it can bring!

It might be useful to take a peek at the notes you made around the beginning of this book. You might even feel like making a new list. Your body is amazing, and it's what takes you through life. We can often take our bodies for granted, so it's nice to remind ourselves of how wonderful it is to be able to do all the things we want it to do.

♥ Find out what your passions are . . . and nurture them!

Do what you love, whether that's coding or writing poetry— or both! Try out different activities and see what brings you the most joy. Finding the things you like to do and are good at helps build self-esteem—as well as a more positive image of yourself and your body.

♥ Be kind to yourself!

Make a habit of encouraging yourself and try some "self-talk," saying nice things like: "Job well done," "Wow, I'm strong," and "I look good in this top!" And when things don't work out the way you hoped? Try saying: "I didn't make it this time, but I'll figure out another way to succeed the next chance I get!" Studies have shown that self-talk really does work and can change the way you see yourself. So feel free to compliment and admire yourself as much as you like!

💜 Move your body all around!

Physical activity and sports are an ideal way of gathering joy from the movement of your body and appreciating what it's capable of! This is also an important part of body positivity, and we'll talk more about it in Chapter 9.

🖤 Take care of your friendships and other relationships.

We should surround
ourselves with people
who support us and
make us feel good about
ourselves. If someone
you are friends with doesn't
feel supportive of your feelings,
it's okay to look for other friends
who are more in alignment with your thoughts and feelings.
Friendships change all the time, and it doesn't mean something is wrong with you if you no longer get along with those
you have been friends with.

🖤 Keep shame at bay

If you feel like something about your appearance or your body
makes you feel ashamed in some way, take note of it. If you
can, try and confide in someone you trust about it. Shame
is a thing that feeds on silence, so talking about shameful
things is like a needle that can help pop it, like a balloon. After
all, there's nothing inherently shameful about our bodies.

💜 Become your own number-one fan!

The one person who can give you the most joy and support is you, especially when things get tough. You can be your own best friend and cheer yourself on each day!

💜 Try not to compare yourself to others.

If you notice that you've started to judge yourself based on your impression of someone else, try to shift your attention to something else, such as drawing or having a conversation with someone around you. Read a book or listen to a song you like (an upbeat one, preferably). Later on, you can try the following exercise: think about all the things you are good at and what you like most about yourself.

💜 Don't wallow in worry.

If something is bothering you or you feel anxious or sad about something—and it feels like it will never end—don't keep these feelings bottled up. Find someone you trust to talk about what you're feeling at home or at school. You can write it down in a journal. You can also use your body to get some of these emotions out, like running or dancing out your sadness or anger.

♥ Scroll with care

When you're on social media, pay attention to who you're following and what you're looking at. If you notice that certain posts make you feel anxious or bad about yourself, simply unfollow that person or set your phone aside for some time. Make sure you check and see whether taking a break from social media really does help you feel a bit better overall. And don't forget that what you see on social media is just a piece of someone's life and that photos can be edited, so what you're seeing may not be the full picture.

🖤 Spread the word

When you're feeling good about yourself, it's also nice to share that positivity with others. When giving compliments, try to focus on the person's abilities rather than their appearance. For instance: "You're so smart. What you said was great." Sometimes it's enough to say: "I'm really happy to see you."

🖤 Remember that body positivity is natural!

Feeling good about yourself is a source of joy and satisfaction.

CHAPTER 6

The Body Below the Belt

Ahoy! Let's set off on this body-positive
exploratory mission of the female reproductive
system! In other words, we're talking about
your vagina and the other parts related to it.

On the next few pages, we will go through a bunch of information and vocabulary that might be quite new to you. You don't have to read it all at once—feel free to browse and pick and choose the pieces that seem like they might be the most useful or interesting. The aim here is to explain everything as clearly as possible, but sometimes subjects related to the body can seem strange and complicated at first. So, it's important to give yourself time.

We'll start with the basic science that deals with the human body. Anatomy is the study of the body's structures and organs. And it seems like figuring out how our bodies are built is a good place to start, right? After all, knowledge is power!

External reproductive organs

These are the parts of your reproductive system found outside the body. These parts are also called the genitals or vulva.

❋ **Mons pubis**—A mound of fatty tissue between the skin and the pubic bones that cushions this sensitive area

❋ **Labia majora**—The two outer folds of skin that surround the labia minora and the vaginal opening. These labia are covered in pubic hair.

❋ **Labia minora**—The two inner folds of skin around the vaginal opening

❋ **Vaginal opening**—The outer part of the vagina and where menstrual blood flows out during a period

❋ **Perinium**—A thin area of skin between the vaginal opening and the anus

❋ **Urethra**—The small canal that urine comes out of when we pee

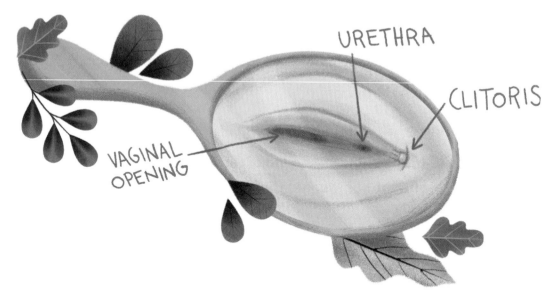

URETHRA

CLITORIS

VAGINAL OPENING

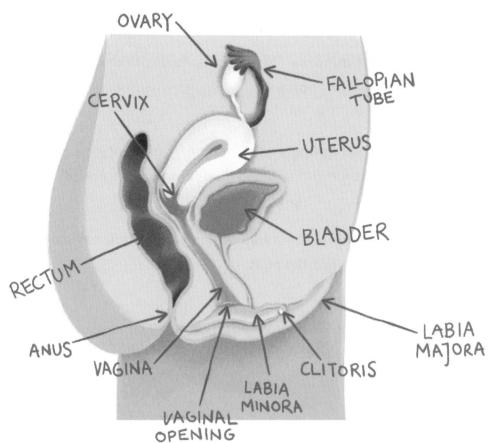

OVARY

FALLOPIAN TUBE

CERVIX

UTERUS

BLADDER

RECTUM

ANUS

VAGINA

CLITORIS

LABIA MAJORA

LABIA MINORA

VAGINAL OPENING

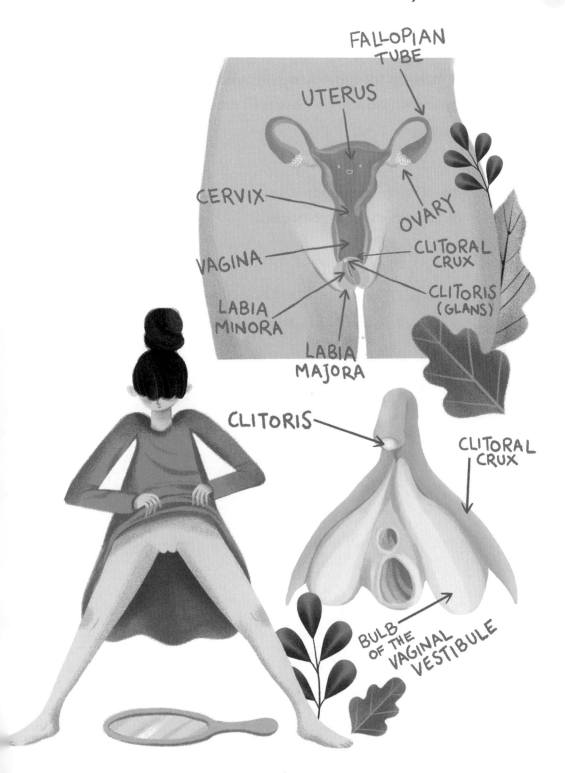

FALLOPIAN TUBE

UTERUS

CERVIX

OVARY

VAGINA

CLITORAL CRUX

LABIA MINORA

CLITORIS (GLANS)

LABIA MAJORA

CLITORIS

CLITORAL CRUX

BULB OF THE VAGINAL VESTIBULE

- **Clitoris crux**—A cluster of tissues and nerve endings that make up the most sensitive part of a woman's body and whose sole purpose is to provide sensory pleasure

- **Anus**—The opening where the gastrointestinal tract ends and stool (poop) comes out

Internal reproductive organs—side and frontal views

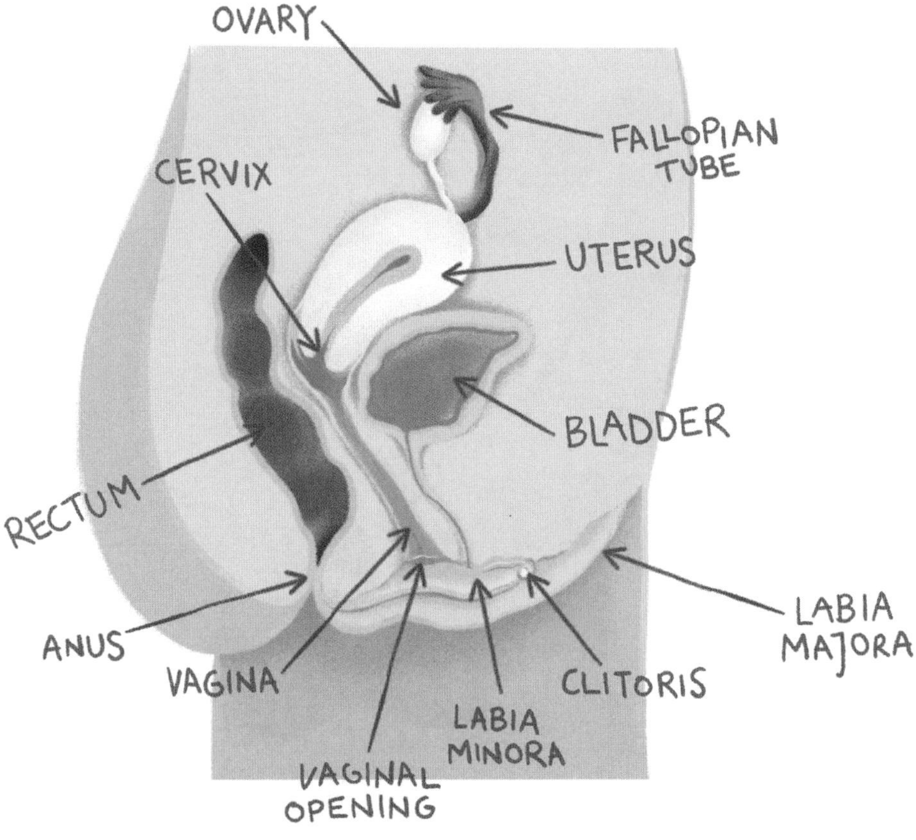

A super-magnified diagram of the clitoris.

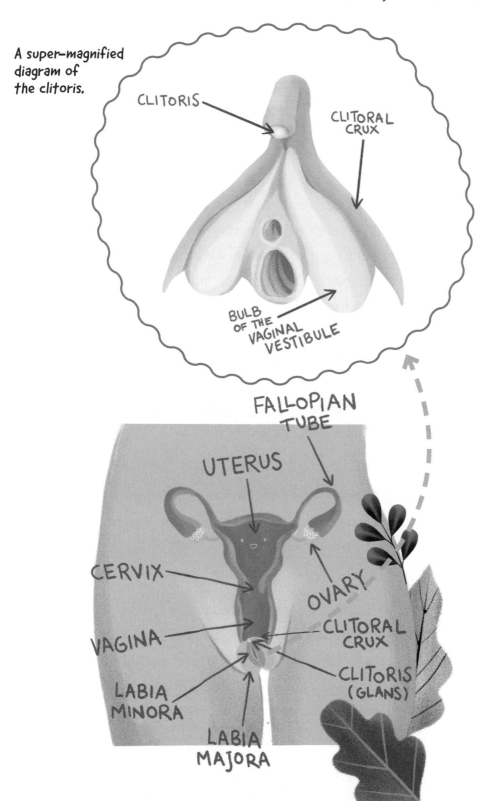

CLITORIS

CLITORAL CRUX

BULB OF THE VAGINAL VESTIBULE

FALLOPIAN TUBE

UTERUS

CERVIX

OVARY

CLITORAL CRUX

VAGINA

CLITORIS (GLANS)

LABIA MINORA

LABIA MAJORA

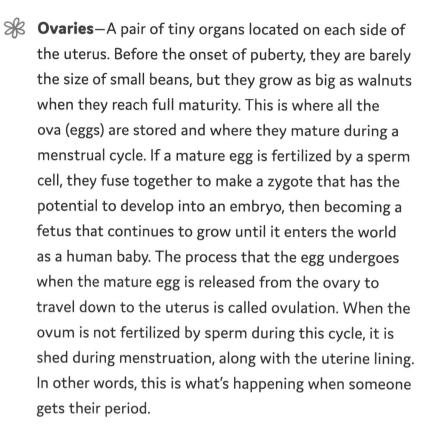 **Ovaries**—A pair of tiny organs located on each side of the uterus. Before the onset of puberty, they are barely the size of small beans, but they grow as big as walnuts when they reach full maturity. This is where all the ova (eggs) are stored and where they mature during a menstrual cycle. If a mature egg is fertilized by a sperm cell, they fuse together to make a zygote that has the potential to develop into an embryo, then becoming a fetus that continues to grow until it enters the world as a human baby. The process that the egg undergoes when the mature egg is released from the ovary to travel down to the uterus is called ovulation. When the ovum is not fertilized by sperm during this cycle, it is shed during menstruation, along with the uterine lining. In other words, this is what's happening when someone gets their period.

Fallopian tubes—A pair of thin tunnels that join the ovaries to the uterus, allowing the egg to travel from the ovaries to the uterus.

Uterus—A muscular organ located in the female pelvis, shaped like an avocado or an upside-down pear. The uterus has a remarkable ability to stretch just like a balloon. Its walls are thick and flexible so that a fetus may have room to develop during pregnancy.

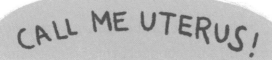

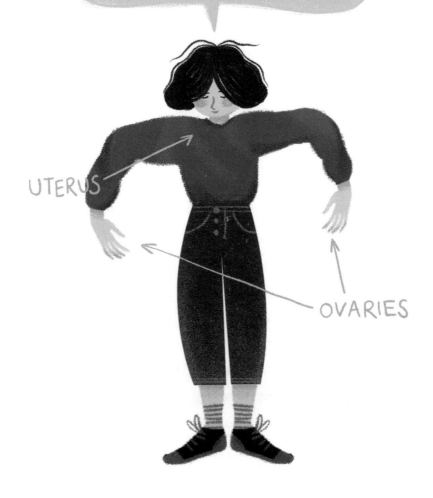

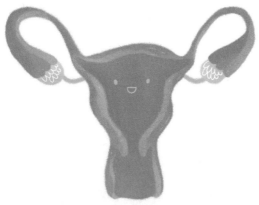

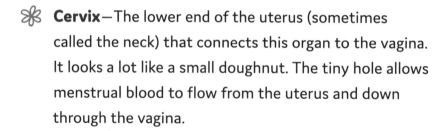 **Cervix**—The lower end of the uterus (sometimes called the neck) that connects this organ to the vagina. It looks a lot like a small doughnut. The tiny hole allows menstrual blood to flow from the uterus and down through the vagina.

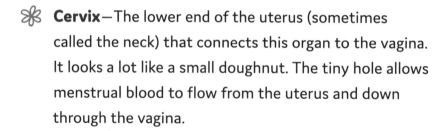 **Vagina**—The canal that connects the cervix and uterus to the outside of the body. When you have your period, the menstrual blood flows out of the vagina. When a baby is born, it usually enters the world through the vaginal opening.

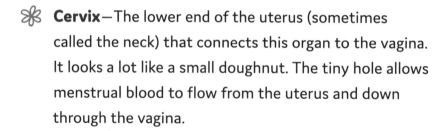 **Clitoral crura** (singular: crux)—A pair of tissues on each side of the vagina that connect the clitoris glans to the inner clitoral region. The glans itself is the cluster of nerve endings at the very center of the crura, at the top of the vulva (just beneath the clitoral hood).

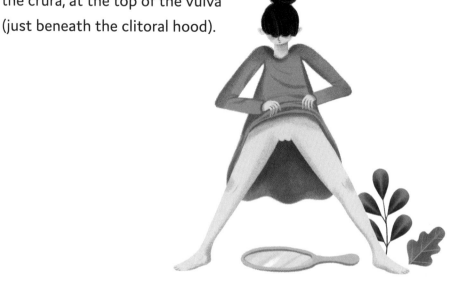

No pressure

When you are going to pee or poo, try not to force or strain yourself. When you're sitting on the toilet, try not to push down. Your body works best when it is relaxed, so try to sit back and let nature take its course.

What is fertility, and how does life begin?

Fertility describes the physical ability to produce off-spring (a.k.a. children). Puberty is the developmental process that prepares a body for this possibility in the future. The life of every human being on Earth starts with the joining together of an egg and a sperm cell. It's as if two puzzle pieces come together to make a whole. Each month, one egg (although sometimes it can be two or even three) develops in the ovaries and travels down through the fallopian tubes to the uterus, where it awaits fertilization. Fertilization happens when there is sperm available to join together with the egg. Now, how does the sperm get there? When a man and woman have sexual intercourse (have sex, make love, or any other phrase people use to describe it), the man places his erect penis in the woman's vagina. He may then release his sperm (called an ejaculation) into her body during sex.

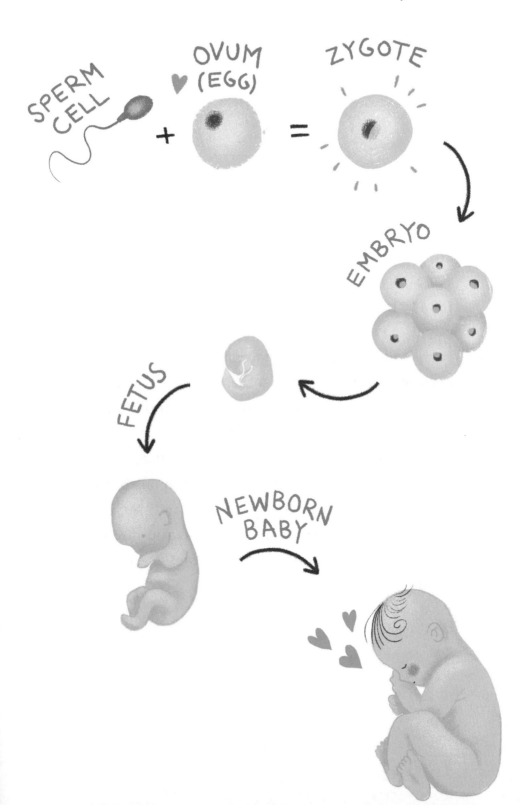

SPERM CELL

+

OVUM (EGG)

=

ZYGOTE

EMBRYO

FETUS

NEWBORN BABY

When two people engage in sexual intercourse, they tend to feel a certain attraction toward one another (sort of like a magnet to a fridge and vice versa). This attraction can be so strong that the two individuals want to get as close as possible to each other. They want to hug, kiss, and touch each other in an intimate way that feels good for both of them. When this intimacy leads to sex, the woman will let the man put his penis in her vagina, and eventually he will release millions of sperm cells that travel up through the cervix and into the uterus, where the egg is waiting. If that couple is not using birth control (which includes different methods of avoiding pregnancy), then one of the sperm cells may fuse with the egg, implant itself into the wall of the uterus, and start to develop through the various stages from a zygote to a fetus—and ultimately a baby.

Babies are usually born between the 37th and 40th week of pregnancy, but it can also happen earlier or later. The baby will then enter the world through the mother's vagina (or through an incision in the abdomen if it is a C-section birth). You, me, and everyone else came about in just this way. And in order to give birth to us, our parents' bodies had to go through the process that prepares the body to produce offspring. This process is called puberty.

CHAPTER 7

First Periods

Menstruation (a.k.a. monthly periods) describes the regular cycle of bleeding when the egg is not fertilized and the uterus sheds it, along with the lining of the uterus. Let's take a look at the diagram in the previous chapter and trace how the period blood flows down through the vagina. You can even take a mirror and look at your own vulva and vaginal opening. It's always good to be familiar with your body and what goes on with it.

What's the point of having periods?

Menstruation is a signal from the body that it is equipped to become pregnant—that is, if and when a woman decides that she indeed wants to have a child. The blood that flows out of the vagina is part of the normal cycle of changes that the body goes through as the egg is released from one or both of the ovaries each month. In this chapter, we'll take a closer look at this process.

When does the first period happen?

Girls usually get their first period between nine and sixteen years old. Some girls get their first period at eleven, some at fourteen, and so on. This is perfectly normal and depends on the individual. After all, puberty is not a sprint!

How long does a period last?

Most periods last about three to five days (although this can vary, and they can be shorter or longer) and repeat about every four weeks (a menstrual cycle typically lasts about 28 days—but we'll come back to this later). During this time, menstrual blood flows out of the vagina. Women continue to menstruate until they are about 50 years of age. That's a pretty big chunk of time!

When do periods stop?

The menstrual cycle can be interrupted or stop altogether for a number of reasons, for instance, during pregnancy. Several weeks after birth, the menstrual cycle will start up again (although breastfeeding may delay it for a longer time).

Some women never get their periods because of hormonal changes or because they have gone through an operation to remove their uterus (known as a hysterectomy). In a healthy body, the absence of a period by a certain age can signal that there might be some irregularity. In these cases, a visit to a doctor specializing in the female reproductive system is recommended. This kind of specialist is called a gynecologist. Of course, all women are advised to see a gynecologist for regular checkups, regardless of how regular (or not) their menstrual cycles are. Women typically stop having periods around 50 years of age, but it can happen a few years earlier or later. The phase of life when a woman is no longer menstruating is called menopause.

What is menopause?

This phase of life is full of changes, and in that way, it is a lot like puberty. This is a unique time in a woman's body when one stage ends and another begins. This is a unique phase in a woman's life when her body goes through substantial changes that are nearly as intense as what girls go through during puberty. Menopause signals that a woman has reached the end of her reproductive years, so her menstruation cycles stop.

Menstruation and womanhood

There are so many ways to be a woman in this world. Some people are born with a female reproductive system and grow up to authentically feel like a girl and eventually a woman. In that case, we say that the person's biological sex assigned at birth matches their identity (or gender). In other words, that person "has a vagina" and "feels like a girl or woman." But sometimes that isn't the case. Someone might be born with a male reproductive system but still feel like a girl or a woman. In our society, these individuals are referred to as transgender. Someone who was assumed to be a male at birth but identifies as a female is said to be a trans girl (or trans woman). This person can decide to change their biological sex by having gender-affirming treatment that allows them to transition into the body that matches their identity. And while some people are born with reproductive systems that clearly appear male or female, others might be born with a more ambiguous anatomy. These individuals are described as intersex, meaning that they may have one or more attributes from both a male and female anatomy. However, if someone who is intersex identifies as a girl or woman, then that is who they are, and their identity should be respected.

Does every woman have a period?

Not necessarily. Trans girls and trans women don't have monthly periods, and sometimes intersex people don't either. Also, people who were either born without a uterus or ovaries or have had all or part of their reproductive system removed do not have periods either.

Do only women have periods?

Once again, not necessarily. Trans boys and men, meaning people who were assumed to be female at birth but identify as male, also have menstrual cycles. Unless they undergo gender-affirming treatments or surgery on their reproductive systems, such individuals will usually continue having a monthly period. People who are intersex may also menstruate.

There is a semantic link between the words "menstru-ation" and "month." It's not a coincidence at all since menstruation happens more or less once a month. Our ancestors paid a lot of attention to the links between the natural world around us and our bodies, which is why they used similar words for these phenomena.

What's also interesting is that these words are also re-lated to the word "moon" as the duration of a month is based on the lunar cycle of a new moon to a full moon. Long ago, people noticed that the moon would appear and disappear in a regular and predictable way—just like the regular bleeding that happens during menstru-ation. Both the lunar cycle and the menstrual cycle last just about 28 days (although some women's cycles can be shorter or longer). It's quite possible that the first women on Earth were able to track their menstrual cy-cles by observing the phases of the moon!

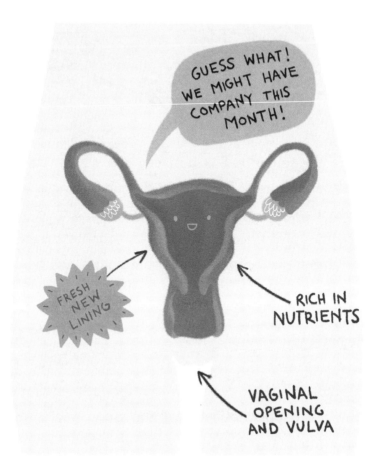

How do periods happen?

Okay, so it might sound a bit complicated at first. Even grown-ups aren't always sure how to explain it very well. Let's try our best to keep it simple, shall we? So, a woman's anatomy is structured in such a way that the uterus prepares to welcome a fertilized egg at every menstrual cycle (just about every month). In other words, every month the body is preparing for a potential pregnancy.

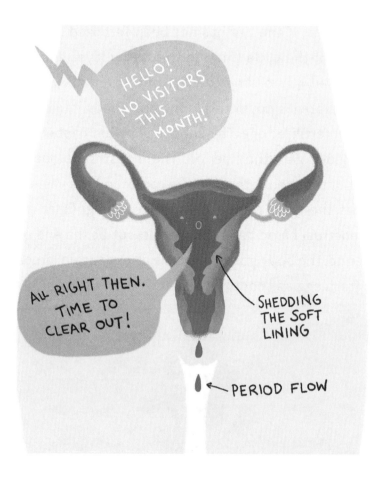

As part of these preparations, the lining of the uterus thickens (a mucous membrane officially known as the endometrium). The purpose of this is to provide the necessary nutrients to an egg that has been successfully fertilized. This lining is like a warm blanket that is meant to cushion and nourish a developing egg—if indeed it does end up getting fertilized during that cycle.

Of course, if the egg has not been fertilized at this key phase in the cycle (making this cushy layer entirely unnecessary), it is time to clear out. In other words, the uterus breaks down this lining and sheds it, along with the unfertilized egg. This shedding is what happens when someone gets their period. The menstrual blood flows out of the uterus, through the cervix and the vagina, and exits the body from the vaginal opening. Once all the menstrual blood has been cleared out at the end of the period, the body starts the cycle all over again, preparing a fresh egg and endometrium.

Menstrual period up close

Periods are just part of a whole series of physical changes a woman's body goes through each month. Just like the full moon is a single phase of the moon cycle, periods are part of the menstrual cycle.

How do periods work?

The following rundown is based on a 28-day cycle, but yours might be a few days longer or shorter. You can also compare the diagram of the menstrual cycle below to the illustration of the lunar phases on the next few pages.

♡ Days 1–4
Season: Winter
Moon phase: New moon

The lining of the uterus is broken down and shed through the vaginal opening as period blood.

How you might be feeling . . .

Like in wintertime, this perhaps can be a time of rest and self-care. You might feel less energetic than usual, and you might experience some aches and pains.

Phases of the moon and the four seasons

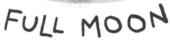

Menstrual cycle

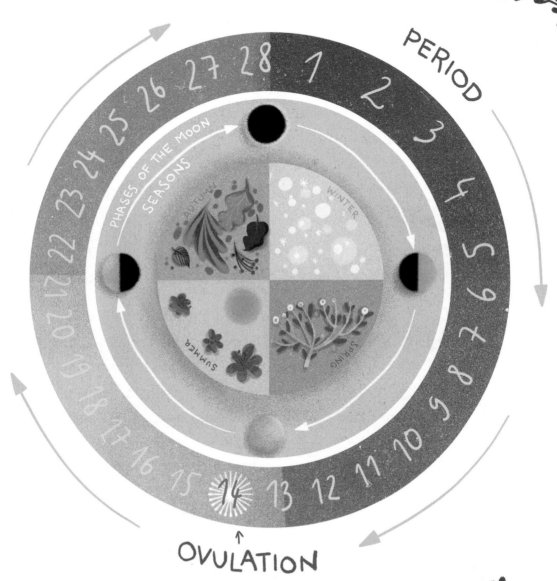

New and notable

It might be a good idea to start tracking how you're feeling on certain days in a journal or notes app. Eventually you might start to notice some regularity in terms of your mood or physical condition, and you might be able to "predict" what's about to come in the next phase of your cycle. This can help you to understand your body better and be more prepared for its monthly changes.

♡ **Days 4–14**
Season: Spring
Moon phase: Second quarter (waxing gibbous)

Even before your period has ended, the pituitary gland is already sending a signal to the ovaries with the message that it's time to get back to work! Time to prepare the next egg! While the ovaries get the egg ready for release, the uterus starts creating a new endometrium (the soft layer lining the uterus). Ovulation is just around the corner!

How you might be feeling . . .

With each new day of this phase in the cycle, you might feel more and more energized and inspired. It's a bit like the burst of spring after the winter.

♡ **Day 14—Ovulation**
Season: Summer
Moon phase: Full moon

The egg is now mature and it begins passing through the fallopian tube and down to the uterus.

How you might be feeling . . .

You may continue to feel more energized during ovulation. You might see the discharge in your underwear becoming thicker, a bit like egg whites. Some girls and women might even see a few drops of blood in this discharge or experience a slight ache in their abdomen during this phase.

♡ **Days 14–28**
Season: Autumn
Moon phase: Third quarter (Waning gibbous)

An unfertilized egg can only survive between 12 to 24 hours, and then it will start to break down. This sends a signal to the uterus that there is no pregnancy and that the lining isn't needed. The cycle is close to the finish line, and the period is about to start again. However, if the egg has been fertilized by a sperm cell in this phase, then the uterus will launch a "pregnancy program" instead of a period. At the start of pregnancy, the cluster of cells implants itself into the soft lining of the uterus and begins to develop.

How you might be feeling . . .

As the first day of your period approaches, your energy levels might start dipping again. You might also feel a bit more irritable or annoyed. The truth is that we don't always have the opportunity to rest when we need it, or we might have to go on with our everyday activities even when we don't feel up to it. Frustration is a natural reaction in this case, and the best thing we can do is to take note of how we are feeling and adapt as best we can.

If it wasn't for menstrual cycles and periods, we wouldn't have people being born every day all over the world. So, there's a great deal of power in menstruation after all.

Your first period

The day a girl gets her first period can be very special. She might get gifts or flowers on that day if that's a custom in her family. Other times, it might just be a day like any other, apart from this unexpected arrival! You might want to ask an older relative or sibling what it was like when they had their first period. You can plan in advance how you'd like to celebrate that day (or not). The most important thing is for you to feel comfortable about what's happening. You might feel quite different, or you might feel exactly the same as before. You might feel a bit sad or disappointed. Let the emotions flow! Getting your first period is a big change in your life. It's something entirely new that might take a while getting used to. You might feel like talking to your friends and other women about what it's like. Whatever makes you feel more at home in this new phase of your life, feel free to do it.

How do you know when you're about to get your first period?

Girls usually get their first period about two or three years after they notice their breasts have started to grow. You might also start to notice a thicker discharge in your underwear with a bit of an acidic smell, which is completely natural. These are all signs that your body is developing according to its natural rhythm. Once you notice these changes, you can expect to get your period in the next twelve months or so. There's also a good chance that you will start menstruating at the same age as your mother did, so find out when that was if you can. This is a good navigational point on your puberty map!

What will my first period feel like? What about my next periods?

Since the menstrual flow is mostly made up of blood, it's usually bright red and thicker than water. You might find jelly-like bits of tissue that come from the endometrium that lines the uterus in the previous phase of the cycle. You may find that the menstrual blood is more brown than red, especially during your first period. The color of menstrual blood can range from a light pink to dark red or brown, and it can change throughout a single period or over the months and years, depending on the individual.

If you look at one of your used tampons or menstrual pads, it might seem like a whole lot of blood comes out during a period. But the reality is that it's not that much at all. Each month, an average of three tablespoons of blood comes out as menstrual bleeding. There are, of course, people who have lighter or heavier periods. If you notice that you have more menstrual blood than you believe is normal, it's good to pay a visit to the doctor to make sure that everything is in order.

Regular and irregular cycles

Doctors usually describe periods using one of two adjectives: regular and irregular. In a "regular" menstrual cycle, you can expect to get your period more or less around the same time each month, meaning it comes after a certain number of days. In an "irregular" cycle, the number of days between periods varies. For instance, there might be 28 days between cycles one month, then as many as 34 days the next, and so on.

Sometimes you might even skip a period once in a while. This is normal for adolescent girls since their bodies are still adapting to these new changes. It might be between 6 to 18 months before the menstrual cycle becomes more regular. Please remember that if you are worried about any aspect of your period or menstrual cycle, you should confide in a trusted adult and possibly ask them to make an appointment for you with the gynecologist (a doctor specializing in the female reproductive system).

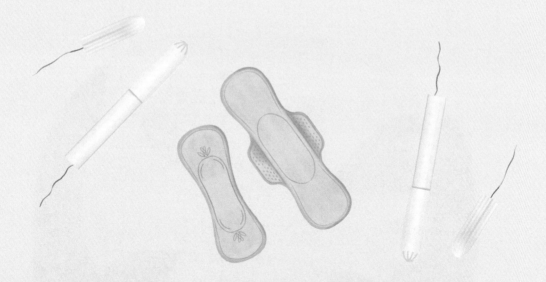

Running the numbers

The average human female ends up menstruating for a total of ten years out of her entire lifetime (i.e., 3,500 days) and can end up using up to 15,000 tampons or pads overall.

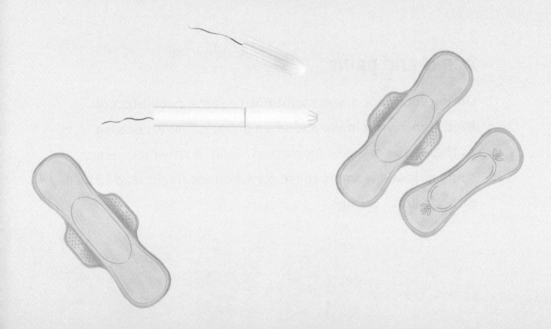

Aches and pains

During your period, you might notice some discomfort or even pain in your lower abdomen or back. This is because as the uterus releases menstrual blood, it contracts. For some girls and women, these contractions might lead to rather painful cramps.

The aches and pains of a period can usually be helped with a regular pain relief medicine. But make sure to ask an adult for advice before taking any medication. If the pain becomes severe, to the point where it's impossible to go about your day in a normal way, make sure to have an adult book you a doctor's appointment.

Other solutions for period pains:

♡ A hot water bottle or heating pad can help soothe most aches (just take care not to burn yourself).

♡ Gentle stretching exercises or a leisurely walk outdoors

♡ A good rest or a nap

♡ Games and laughter

♡ Good company

♡ Basic pain relief medication, such as ibuprofen. But remember to consult an adult before taking any medicine and always follow the guidelines on the leaflet.

Self-care during your period

In the first few days of your period (or even a couple of days before it arrives), you might feel a bit more tired than usual. Try to give yourself the space to relax when you need it.

What's PMS?

These three letters stand for premenstrual syndrome, which describes a set of symptoms that many girls and women experience during this phase in their menstrual cycle. For instance, aches and pains, tense muscles, anxiety, headaches, tenderness in the breasts, etc. If you experience any of these symptoms, you might want to consult your doctor for advice.

Never alone

Can you believe that at one single moment, a total of about 300 million people are menstruating? That's nearly the population of the entire United States! That's a pretty dizzying statistic, right?

Pads, tampons, and more

There's a whole bunch of products out there to avoid messing up your underwear when you're having your period. Pads, tampons, cups, and other popular items can be used to collect or absorb your menstrual blood. You can ask a trusted adult to show you what your options are.

Did you know . . .

Products like pads, tampons, and menstrual cups are not universal, and not everybody around the world uses them. In fact, in many countries, these items are inaccessible to girls and women or are too expensive. For instance, in Zambia, they use the buds from cotton plants to absorb their period blood . . . or even dried-out cow patties! They wrap them up in a clean rag and place them in their underwear just like a regular pad. Cow patties are as absorbent as sponges, so they're very effective at soaking up menstrual blood.

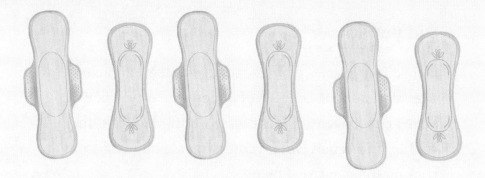

Sanitary pads

These are usually a long strip of soft, absorbent material that you place inside your underwear. There is usually an adhesive strip on the underside to make sure it doesn't slip. Some pads have so-called "wings" that also have adhesive on them to stick to each side of your underwear. This helps the pad stay in place and avoid leaks.

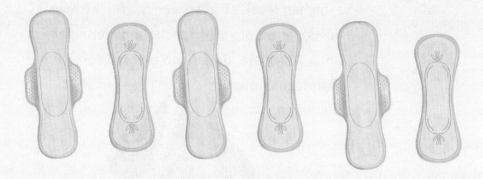

Did you know . . .

In medieval Europe, women most likely bled through their skirts, as the concept of underwear as we know it hadn't been invented yet. It wasn't until the late 19th century that a belt was invented to hold up a pad to soak up the menstrual blood.

Pad absorbency

Sanitary pads come in a range of absorbencies, which refers to the amount of menstrual blood that the material can soak up. This is usually indicated using the symbol of a drop, with one drop indicating a low absorbency and up to four drops indicating a higher level of absorbency (for heavier flows). There are also special pads for nighttime, which are longer and more absorbent than regular pads.

It's important to change your pad regularly through-out the day, at least every two or three hours. In the nighttime, you can leave it for the entire time you're sleeping—unless your periods are especially heavy (and this might be something you want to consult with your doctor about). When you get up in the morning, you might feel a sudden rush as the blood that accumulated during the night flows out due to gravity.

Tampons

This tube of absorbent material is placed inside the vagina, with a little string left hanging outside your body. The tampon absorbs the menstrual blood before it has a chance to flow out of your body. To remove the tampon, you relax your muscles and gently pull on the string.

Some people prefer to use tampons or find them useful for certain activities such as swimming. It's important to remember to wash your hands before you change your tampon, and make sure to replace it every three to four hours.

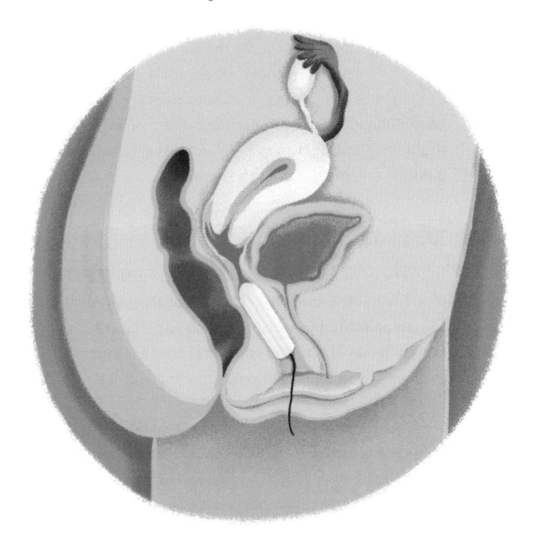

Types of tampons

Like pads, tampons come in a range of absorbencies, from low to high. There are also two types of tampons according to how they are inserted.

♡ Tampons with an applicator include a small tube that helps move the tampon up into the right spot in the vagina.

♡ Tampons without an applicator have no tube and instead you just use your finger to move it into place.

If you want to get started using tampons, try out the smallest ones first—usually marked as "low flow." The smaller the tampon, the easier it is to practice putting it in correctly.

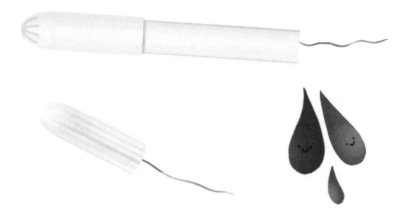

Q&A

Can a tampon get lost up there?

No worries, your tampon is safe and sound! The narrow channel of the vagina ends with the cervix, and its opening is too small for a tampon to pass through. This means the tampon stays in place no matter how much you move around.

How do you insert a tampon without an applicator?

1. Start by washing your hands.
2. Take a breath and relax your muscles. You might want to crouch down or put one foot up on a stool or the toilet bowl.
3. Take the tampon out of the packaging and use your index finger to push it up into place in your vagina.
4. Stand up and check if you can still feel the tampon. If so, try pushing it a bit further until you can't feel it anymore.

How do I remove the tampon?

1. Wash your hands.
2. Take a breath and relax your muscles.
3. Gently tug the string sticking out of your vagina, and it should slowly slip out. Wrap it in a piece of toilet paper and throw it into the trash.

What is toxic shock?

You may have heard about this syndrome before. It's a rare but dangerous condition that can be caused by certain bacteria accumulating in the body. In some cases, it has been linked to tampon use, that is, when a tampon has been left inside the body for too long. To reduce the risk of toxic shock, make sure to use the right absorbency level for your flow (in other words, don't use high-absorbency tampons if you have a relatively light flow) and make sure to change them regularly (at least every 3–4 hours during the day).

Menstrual cups

These are tiny little cups that can be inserted into the vagina to collect period blood. After a couple of hours, you carefully remove the cup, clean it, and then reinsert it. These cups can be used multiple times and every month—for up to 15 years! So, using a menstrual cup is a great way to reduce waste. For younger girls who have recently gotten their first period, there are special mini cups that are easier to insert. It may be a bit tricky at first, but once you get the hang of it, it's a breeze. The thing to remember with menstrual cups is that you need access to a sink to clean the cup properly before you reinsert it.

Reusable sanitary pads

They're not disposable, so they help reduce waste because you can use them multiple times. These pads are usually made of cotton and can be cleaned in the washing machine.

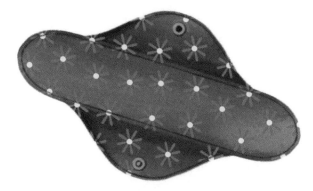

Did you know . . .

Your grandmother probably didn't use tampons or pads because it just wasn't common back in the day. Women used to sew their own period pads, or they'd just use cotton or another naturally absorbent cloth. The period products we know today didn't become popular until around the 1980s and '90s.

Period panties

This is a special kind of underwear with a built-in pad that absorbs menstrual blood. You simply clean your period panties in the washing machine and use them again. This is a great option for girls and women who are especially active or who have a disability. It's also a great backup for other methods for people who have a heavy flow. There's a whole range of period panties in stores and online.

Toss it in the trash, not the toilet!

When you're changing your tampon or pad, make sure not to drop the used ones in the toilet as it can block the pipes and cause a plumbing disaster. Even if it doesn't, it can end up polluting the water supply, since some of these products are made of plastic that takes hundreds of years to break down and can potentially harm wildlife.

So what do I do with it instead?

You can simply wrap your used pad or tampon in toilet paper and throw it into the trash can or a special receptacle for menstrual products. If you find yourself in a bathroom or stall with neither of these (it happens), then wrap it up and throw it into the nearest trash you can find.

Leaks and stains

Sometimes your period flow can be unpredictable. It might arrive unexpectedly in the day or night. Your pad might move around, or your flow might get heavier all of a sudden. Leaks and stains are a normal part of having a period. It happens to everybody, and while it can be pretty annoying, it's nothing to be embarrassed about.

A laughing matter

You might notice that when you laugh or sneeze during your period, you feel a sudden gush. This is because the muscles of your diaphragm and belly are tensing up and pressing on the uterus so that the flow gets momentarily heavier. If you want to try to avoid this unruly effect, you can try to take control over the muscles of your pelvic floor and "pull them up." Granted, it takes a bit of concentration and coordination, but it is a skill that can be acquired (some people even take lessons). But do remember to relax your muscles again afterward!

The smell of it

The smell of menstrual blood is often described as metallic (given its iron content). You might also notice your pad or tampon may have a somewhat unpleasant smell, usually when it comes into contact with air. To control its intensity, make sure to change your disposable period products often. Reusable pads are usually made of cotton or bamboo, naturally absorbent materials that are less prone to strong smells. Menstrual cups keep the blood contained until the moment it is spilled out, so this is an option that reduces the potential for smelly undies. It's important to remember that it's normal for your body to have different smells, and washing regularly can keep these smells at a healthy level.

Period packs

You might find it useful to prepare yourself a "period pack." In other words, a cosmetics bag filled with useful items so that you can be ready when your period arrives. These items can include your favorite period product(s), along with cleansing towelettes and hand sanitizer. Take anything you might need if you find yourself in a spot with no toilet paper or running water. You don't have to carry it around everywhere you go, but it can be useful around the time you expect to get your period. It's also useful to keep a pad in your purse or backpack for unexpected flows—it might come in handy for you or a classmate!

Menstrual calendar

It's easier to manage your period when you know when it's coming, so a menstrual calendar can help you keep track of your cycle. Take a basic calendar or planner and jot down the days you have your period. This will help you figure out the length of your cycle in days so you can start figuring out more or less when you can expect it to come the following month. You can also mark down the other phases of your cycle using the information and illustrations on the previous pages.

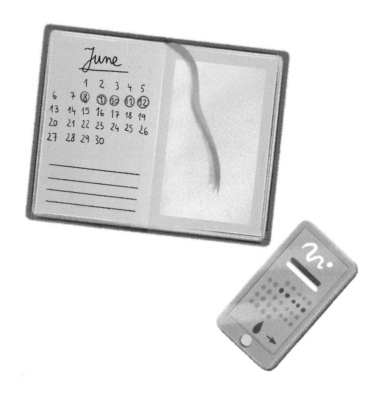

There are plenty of apps out there to help girls and women track their menstrual cycles. The most important aspect of apps like this is privacy. In other words, that means the app developer is not sharing their users' personal data with anyone else. After all, your personal business is precious and belongs to you! If you're interested in using an app, ask a trusted adult to help you find one that is secure and keeps its user data confidential.

Did you know...

Historically, women had fewer periods than they do today. This is not only because they didn't live as long, but they also had more pregnancies and also tended to breastfeed for an extended amount of time (which delays the return of the menstrual cycle). Today, our society has access to modern forms of birth control that can prevent pregnancy. This gives people more control over if and when they want to have children.

Menstruation and exercise

Your period shouldn't be an obstacle in staying active if you want to. As long as you're up for it, you can play sports and take part in gym class. The most important thing is to feel comfortable, starting with the period products that are the most effective for your needs. You might also find it useful to wear period panties either on their own or as a backup.

If you start to feel tired or uncomfortable while playing sports or during gym class, make sure to tell your instructor and take a break if you need to. You might also want to discuss this with a parent so you can be prepared with an action plan in such situations.

Keeping clean

Is it necessary to bathe or shower more often when you have your period? The truth is that a daily shower should suffice, but if you feel the need to have an extra wash (for instance, if you're using pads), then feel free. The most important thing is that you feel fresh and comfortable. Also, remember that you only need to wash the outer parts of your vulva. Your vagina is built to clean itself and doesn't need any extra help.

Can people tell that
I'm menstruating?

No one will know that you have
your period unless you tell them!

Period taboos

A taboo is something that people in a particular society don't talk about (usually without explaining why). The word comes from Polynesia and is used to refer to something that is "sacred." This includes the topic of menstruation. Cultural anthropologists (scientists who study the history of human cultures and customs) believe that menstruation was once a taboo subject because people didn't understand why or how it happened. They might have thought it was a type of magic and perhaps were even fearful of it. That's why they preferred not to talk about it, along the lines of the character known as "He Who Must Not Be Named" from the Harry Potter series. This idea that we shouldn't talk about periods is still around, and there are a lot of people out there who are too shy or embarrassed to talk about the subject.

Let's talk about periods

Having conversations about menstruation is important and healthy. However, in some circles, there is still a lot of silence around the topic, either at home, at school, or in the community. So, bringing it up can sometimes feel challenging. It can take guts. If you find yourself in this kind of situation, try not to feel discouraged. Often, it's just because they've been raised to not talk about it. This book might be a good conversation starter if there's someone you think you might want to discuss your period with.

Period poverty

There's a whole bunch of menstrual products out there—tampons, pads, wipes, panty liners, etc. And the truth is that there are millions of girls and women in the world who can't afford to buy these items. A lot of times they might be faced with the choice of using their money for pads or to buy food. There are about 500 million people across the globe who don't have access to menstrual products.

Over an entire lifetime, the average woman who tends to only use menstrual pads during her period will end up spending about $5,000 on these items. Then there are the other related costs, such as pain relief medication and so on.

There are also a lot of girls out there who are so embarrassed about menstruation that they get anxious even asking their parents to buy them the items they need. They don't need to be embarrassed! The more you talk about it, the more it becomes a topic people aren't afraid to speak up about.

Did you know . . .

In some countries, pads, tampons, and even menstrual cups are available for free. For instance, Scotland became the first country in the world to introduce a law that schools must provide such items for their students. The former prime minister of New Zealand Jacinda Ardern declared in 2020 that her government would also make these products freely available in schools so girls who couldn't afford them wouldn't have to miss school.

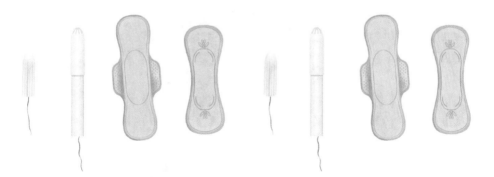

The good news is that there are more and more individual activists and organizations whose goal is to provide menstrual products to people in need. In the U.S., nonprofit organizations such as the Alliance for Period Supplies and PERIOD are working to make period products available for free in schools across the country. Also, 17 U.S. states (plus Washington, D.C.) have introduced legislation to combat period poverty by ensuring students have free access to period products. This is a big deal, and the fact that more people are openly talking about periods has made it possible to break taboos and find solutions for period-related issues. Talking about menstruation can be life-changing!

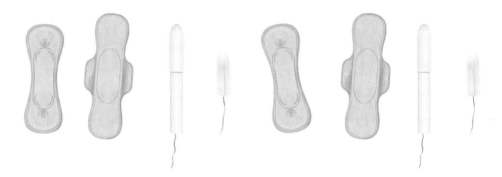

Seeing a specialist

Around the time you get your first period, it is good to make plans for your first appointment with a gynecologist (doctor specializing in female anatomy and reproduction). A gynecologist's job is to make sure a woman's reproductive health is on track, including her uterus, ovaries, vagina, and breasts. At your first appointment, you will find out the details of puberty from an anatomical sense and more about the structure of a woman's

reproductive system. You can also feel free to ask any question. Basically, your gynecologist is your personal medical advisor for all matters to do with puberty and menstruation. Not too shabby, right?

It's normal for someone to be nervous about their first gynecological appointment. Sometimes choosing a woman gynecologist can make things easier. Think about whether the gender of your doctor is important to you and ask a parent or guardian to find a doctor who specializes in treating girls and young women.

During your visit, the doctor will ask you questions about your period to determine whether your cycle is regular. So, it will be handy to have this information ready, such as the date of your first period (when it started and when it finished) and how you were feeling.

Remember, if it makes you feel more comfortable, you can have a trusted family member accompany you to your appointment.

Parental consent

In the U.S., the rules about whether a minor (under 18 years of age) can see a doctor without their parent's permission vary from state to state. In most states, minors can get a gynecological exam without parental consent, but they might need to get consent if they require further treatment.

(Just a few) reasons why you should make an appointment to see a gynecologist:

⟫ Getting a first period before the age of 9

⟫ Not getting a first period by age 16

⟫ No sign of breast development by age 13

⟫ A pause of three months or more between periods

⟫ A menstrual cycle that is shorter than 21 days or longer than 45

⟫ Unusual spotting (bleeding) between periods

⟫ Unusual bleeding, abdominal pain, or other unusual symptoms

⟫ A period that lasts longer than 7 days

⟫ Excessively heavy periods (changing a pad more frequently than every two hours and needing to change them at night)

Big feelings

Getting your first period is a humongous change in your life. It can be stressful at first, just like anything that's new and unfamiliar. Learning about your menstrual cycle and how it all works for you takes time. But you'll get there! By following your own cycle, you'll discover your individual, unique rhythm.

There are plenty of women who enjoy the time when they get their period. It's a moment when they feel like they can take a moment to rest and spend some time alone. There are also some women who feel energized during their periods. It's all relative. The most important thing is to observe your own cycle and how you feel during this time.

CHAPTER 8

Taking Care of Yourself During Puberty

You already know that puberty is a time of so much change—in your body as well as in your mind and heart. That's why it's important to focus on treating yourself right—with love and care. Your wondrous body is putting a lot of work into taking you through the transformation of puberty. Give it your kindness, support, and care. Learning self-care is a key skill, and it's worth nurturing this skill over the course of your entire life.

✐ 1. Sleeping beauty

At this point in your life, you need a minimum of 8 to 9 hours of sleep per night. This is when the real magic happens: the cells of your body rest and regenerate, while the brain puts all the information it has collected throughout the day into order. It also releases growth hormone (it's true—your growing happens while you're asleep!) and your immune system carries out a general inspection, fighting any bugs that might have snuck in. All in all, the truth is that good sleep is golden!

⌀ 2. Laugh it up

There's something magical about laughter. Not only does it instantly improve your mood, but it can improve the moods of others around you thanks to its "infectious" qualities. Try to find a couple of reasons to laugh each day. It can be anything from a dad joke (or a mom joke) to joking around with your friends or siblings. Or check out some cute pet videos online!

A valuable skill—but one that's not easy to acquire—is the ability to laugh at oneself. This means, of course, taking a light-hearted approach to things (but not to be confused with making fun of yourself) and treating yourself with kindness and compassion.

Laughter is so important because it helps you breathe more deeply, sending a signal to your nervous system that you are safe and it's okay to relax. Plus, a good belly laugh helps with digestion because it gives your guts a little massage. And it can also help loosen up the whole body and calm the mind. There's nothing but goodness in having a hearty chuckle!

3. Taste the rainbow

Let's go back to one of the things we talked about at the very beginning of this book. Remember when we said that your body is like a home and during puberty that home is getting bigger, so you need the right building materials? In other words, it's vital to eat the right foods, especially the sort that build bones and muscle, like calcium and protein. Cheese, eggs, beans, and nuts are good sources of these nutrients.

And the more fruits and vegetables you eat, the better. And it's even better to consume a wide variety across all the colors of the rainbow. For instance, in a single day, you can try to have an apple (red), a plum (purple), a banana (yellow), some spinach (green), and some carrots (orange).

Of course, it's impossible to get by on just fruits and vegetables. We also need grains, proteins, and fats in our diets. Food is supposed to be a source of sustenance, but also of great joy, too! For fun, try to focus on the taste, smell, and texture of the foods you eat—that can also bring you more enjoyment while eating.

4. Hug it out

Cuddling is an ancient way of communicating that people have used since before the time we started using words. Touch is incredibly powerful because it creates a bond that holds us together. That bond helps us to be kinder to each other and take better care of one another.

Cuddles and hugs help the body and brain relax while making us feel safer. Scientists even say that regular close contact can boost the immune system.

🖋 5. Think about starting a journal

Remember those lined pages you started to fill up at the beginning of the book? If you enjoyed putting your thoughts down on paper, you might want to do it more often. You can write notes to yourself and your body as a way of organizing all the thoughts you've been having lately. Maybe write about the sorts of things you have been noticing about yourself, how you feel, and what's been changing in and around you. You can also draw pictures or fill the space up with stickers.

Many girls and young women keep diaries as a way of connecting with themselves, understanding their feelings, and creating a souvenir of this time in their lives to look back on when they're older.

6. Check on yourself and what you're feeling

All the emotions and feelings, and even thoughts you experience, will have some effect on your body. When we're angry, we might clench our fists and jaw while our heart starts racing. Joy feels like a warm rush in the belly. Fear makes us want to shrink down and disappear. It's good to understand how our body responds to certain things because it can give us the ability to understand ourselves and our reactions a lot better.

A nice idea might be to create your own nighttime ritual. When you're in bed and getting ready to drift off to sleep, try asking your body how it's feeling, focusing on one part at a time. For example, you can start with the big toe of your left foot. After each question, take a pause and listen to the reply. You might feel warmth, cold, vibration, tingling—or nothing at all! That's totally normal. Sometimes it takes a while to hear your inner voice (another name for that intuition or gut instinct you feel sometimes). Even if you never hear your body respond to your questions, it's always good to have a bit of quiet time once in a while.

7. Move your body

Do you have a particular sport you enjoy—or any other physical activity you can't imagine doing without? It's wonderful to have something you want to do on a regular basis—a way to move your body and feel good. If you don't have a favorite activity, maybe see what some of your friends enjoy and try their favorites with them. You may just fall in love with the activity as well! Remember, your body was built to move! And the more you move, the easier it gets to keep it up. The more you stretch, the more flexible your body gets! Movement helps nourish your body, improve circulation, and distribute the energy you get from the foods you eat! Physical activity can also boost your mood and self-esteem because when your body is in motion, you release "feel-good" hormones called endorphins.

The truth is that sometimes gym classes are more of a pain than joy. You might not be a fan of track or dodgeball, and that's okay! Your physical education teachers are just trying to get you moving and introduce you to a number of different activities you might not have tried on your own. There might be other forms of exercise out there that might be right for you. Think about what kind of sport or exercise you might want to do outside of school: swimming, dancing, riding your bike, skateboarding, rollerblading—and there's so much more!

A few simple ways to stay active after school

🌸 Running

🌸 Riding a bike

🌸 Jumping rope

🌸 Practicing dance routines from YouTube (or make your own choreography)

🌸 Throwing a frisbee

🌸 Tossing a ball around or playing basketball

8. Find your tribe

Your number-one tribe might be your family, but as you get older, your friends start to play a bigger role in your life. It's not always easy to figure out who the right friends are for you, but it's important to surround yourself with people you can trust and who make you feel good about yourself.

CHAPTER 9

How Long Does Puberty Last?

Sometimes, when the adults around you find out you got your first period, they might say something like, "Congratulations! You're a woman now!" But it's really not that simple. After all, when you're 11, 12, 13, and 14—you're not an adult yet. And that's perfectly fine because there's no need to rush these things. You're the only one who knows what feels right for you.

Getting your first period isn't exactly a magic spell that works instantly to transform a girl into a woman. As we know very well, growing up is a gradual process that happens over a series of phases and over many years. And even though in our society a person is considered an adult at 18, scientists have shown that the brain doesn't fully mature until someone is about 25 years old. Puberty is just the start of developing into a full-grown, mature human being. The truth is that growing up lasts a lifetime, through all the various steps of getting to know yourself, others, and the world around you and gaining knowledge, self-confidence, and independence.

Talk to an adult you trust and ask them when it was that they finally felt they were truly grown up. What was the thing that made them feel like they had finally achieved adulthood? What was the moment that really changed things for them? You can ask any number of people, from your parents, grandparents, aunts, uncles, and cousins. You can find out plenty of interesting things from the people just around you. And asking these questions and having conversations will also help you get closer and get to know each other better.

LET'S REMEMBER:
Each person develops at their
own pace and in their own way.
And the path you follow is all yours!

Use this page to jot down a few things that are related to adulthood for you:

♥ ....

♥ ....

♥ ....

♥ ....

♥ ....

♥ ....

♥ ....

♥ ....

♥ ....

♥ ....

♥ ....

♥ ....

♥ ....

♥ ....

♥ ....

♥ ....

♥ ....

♥ ....

♥ ....

♥ ....

♥ ....

Here you can make note of some of the interesting things others have shared with you about their own experiences of growing into adulthood:

♥ ....

♥ ....

♥ ....

♥ ....

♥ ....

♥ ....

♥ ....

♥ ....

♥ ....

♥ ....

♥ ....

♥ ....

♥ ....

♥ ....

♥ ....

♥ ....

♥ ....

♥ ....

♥ ....

♥ ....

♥ ....

Once in a while, you might want to come back and have another look at these notes. And you can always add new ideas whenever they appear. You might even want to cross out certain things that no longer feel valid for you. Cancel, rewrite, rephrase. You are free to do whatever you like on these pages.

The only rule is to go boldly through life and discover all the things hidden around the bend!

Forge your
own path

You can use the following page
to jot down the details of your first
period and keep it as a souvenir.

SPECIAL
MEMENTO PAGE
FOR YOUR
FIRST PERIOD

You can use this page to jot down your thoughts about starting menstruation.

DATE:

PLACE:

HOW I'M FEELING ...

HOW IT HAPPENED ...

WHO I TALKED TO ABOUT IT ...

Jot down some of your dreams
and ambitions:

♥ ....

♥ ....

♥ ....

♥ ....

♥ ....

♥ ....

♥ ....

♥ ....

♥ ....

♥ ....

♥ ....

♥ ....

♥ ....

♥ ....

♥ ....

♥ ....

♥ ....

♥ ....

♥ ....

♥ ....

Make a note of some of your favorite things to do:

♥ ....

♥ ....

♥ ....

♥ ....

♥ ....

♥ ....

♥ ....

♥ ....

♥ ....

♥ ....

♥ ....

♥ ....

♥ ....

♥ ....

♥ ....

♥ ....

♥ ....

♥ ....

♥ ....

♥ ....

List a few things that boost your mood or make you laugh:

♥ ....

♥ ....

♥ ....

♥ ....

♥ ....

♥ ....

♥ ....

♥ ....

♥ ....

♥ ....

♥ ....

♥ ....

♥ ....

♥ ....

♥ ....

♥ ....

♥ ....

♥ ....

♥ ....

♥ ....

Author's acknowledgments

I'd like to express my deep gratitude to the following contributors for their help and support in creating this book:

Ewa Barcz, Alicja Długołęcka, Katarzyna Gałązka, Kasia Jabłońska-Kuśmierek, Małgorzata Kosińska, Karolina Oponowicz, Kamila Raczyńska-Chomyn, Agnieszka Stein, Sylwia Szwed, and Aleksandra Wierzbicka.

I'd also like to thank Ewa Kwiatkowska and Ewa Pietruszczak for trusting me and giving me the space to spread my wings. And to Maciek—for everything.

A big thanks to the community: a dedication to the people who put their trust in moonka from the start, when we were still at the crowdfunding stage. In lending their support, they not only made it possible to publish the first body-positive guide to puberty in our native country of Poland—but confirmed our belief that the greatest strength lies in an engaged community. These are the people who believed that making the facts about puberty accessible to young people is important and necessary. For their trust and support, we'd like to offer our heartfelt and moonlit gratitude:

Krystyna Belka, the Bieluń sisters from Ministerstwa Dobrego Mydła (Ministry of Good Soap), Ania Brzezińska, Arkadiusz Falecki, Łukasz Gaszyński, Maria Górska-Piszek, Anka Jabłońska, Danusia Janiak-Herman, Klaudia Kotowska, Aleksandra and Iliana Kowalczyk, Marta Kozłowska, Aleksandra Mazurek, Ola Leonowicz, Agnieszka Leśny, Doris Nawrot, Anna Nowosad, Katarzyna Orzeszko, Karol and Ewelina Podgórczyk, Agata Rychlik, Maria Ryll, Sebastian Szklarz, Agata Wala, Anna Werner, Konrad Witkowski, Your KAYA, and Roma Zaborowska.

AUTHOR

Barbara Pietruszczak is the co-creator of moonka publishing house and author of books on body–positive puberty. She is a journalist specializing in body image, sexuality, menstruation, taboos, and stereotypes related to the body. On social media, she runs an educational project Pani Miesiączka (Miss Menstruation).

ILLUSTRATOR

Anna Rudak creates graphics for cultural institutions, illustrations for magazines, music labels, packaging, and the fashion and children's industries. She is inspired by colors, moments, and positive associations that she inserts into her works so that they can later resound in new spaces. She lives and works in her hometown of Gdańsk, Poland.

TRANSLATOR

Agnes Monod-Gayraud is a translator and author of children's books, with a focus on non-fiction titles. Winner of the 2016 Best Educational Writing Award from the UK's Society of Authors. She is also a language editor for the Astronomy & Astrophysics academic journal, based at the Paris Observatory. She holds a B.A. in Comparative Literature from New York University and an M.A. in American Cultural Studies from the University of Warsaw. A native New Yorker, she currently lives with her family in London. Her first children's book, *Faedom*, was published in October 2024.

ALSO AVAILABLE

Understanding Adolescence for Boys:
A Body-Positive Guide to Puberty
by Barbara Pietruszczak,
illustrated by Anna Rudak,
translated by Agnes Monod-Gayraud.
ISBN 978-1-64690-042-8

Understanding Adolescence for Boys is a frank discussion about puberty and growing up with a focus on understanding your emotions as changes take place, and creating a positive relationship with your body.

Knowledge of our own bodies is a superpower because it helps us understand what's going on inside of us. This is especially true during adolescence—a time of big changes! Want to understand what puberty and adolescence is all about? This book has answers to all your questions, with plenty of illustrations to help you get to know your body … and yourself, and put you on the path to feeling good in your own skin.